MW01137771

The Queen

Her Majesty Queen Elizabeth II

A Royal Biography

Michael Woodford

Introduction

At some point, when they reach their mid-sixties, most people will accept the ravages of later middle age and gracefully, often gratefully, ease themselves into retirement. Not so the Queen.

At 91 years, Her Majesty, Queen Elizabeth II continues to work hard at her numerous duties for the nation and Commonwealth.

Having held the throne for 65 years, she continues to demonstrate her commitment to fulfilling her various roles – Head of State, figurehead of many charities, Supreme Governor of the Church of England, upholder of the faith for the Church of Scotland.

She may now undertake far fewer trips abroad, but her activities within the United Kingdom remain considerable.

During her reign, there have been highs and lows, but through the divorces, disasters and, sadly, deaths, as well as the joys and jubilees, the Queen has stood firm.

With the support of her husband, Prince Phillip, children Charles, Anne, Andrew and Edward, numerous grandchildren and great grandchildren she has remained an overwhelmingly popular monarch.

How has she achieved this? What enabled her to overcome the tribulations of the '80s and '90s? And why does she remain loved and respected in the hearts of so many?

A Jubilee to Remember

2012 gave the nation a chance to celebrate. Not only was London to hold the Olympic Games, but the year marked the Diamond Jubilee of the Queen. Sixty years of service and leadership were to be celebrated in style.

Central to the occasion would be the Thames River Pageant – a giant flotilla of craft traveling along the waterway from Wandsworth to Tower Bridge. Around a thousand ships, barges and boats took part, with an estimated million people watching from riverbanks. Ten times that number tuned into the BBC to watch their coverage.

The Queen herself, accompanied by Prince Phillip, took part aboard the Spirit of Chartwell, with Tower Bridge's enormous bascules opening to allow the ship to pass beneath.

Not every vessel taking part, however, was as grand as the Royal Barge. 50 or so of the participating craft had, over seventy years previously, braved the tumultuous seas and German bombardments to rescue allied soldiers stranded at Dunkirk.

Amongst them was the Hastings lifeboat, the wonderfully named Cyril and Lilian Bishop. The name was chosen to commemorate Lilian Bishop, a wealthy local lady.

Mrs. Bishop donated £4500 towards the cost of the ship on condition that it was named after herself and her second husband.

She had experienced tragedy when her husband died unexpectedly young. The same fate had also befallen her first husband.

Despite her great wealth, such was her grief that, in the year the lifeboat was launched, she took her own life.

However, prior to this she had also donated a similar sum to the Newhaven lifeboat fund in order that a sister ship could be created to remember her first husband.

This vessel was called The Cecil and Lilian Philpott.

During the evacuation the Hastings lifeboat saved the lives of 51 soldiers, transporting them safely back to England even though it became stuck on sandbanks for four hours.

Lilian Bishop would no doubt have been proud of the achievements of the little ship named in her honour.

Although it had been start of the art for its time, more modern lifeboats came along, rendering it out of date.

With costs of maintenance rising, it was eventually sold and renamed Stenoa by its current owners.

In recognition of Britain's enormous and long naval history, the privately commissioned barge Gloriana was given pride of place at the head of the flotilla.

A mixture of eighteen rowers, including Olympic medalists and military heroes propelled the large, oar-powered boat along the Thames.

The day of the Jubilee celebrations was damp and dreary, but most did not let this get them down. An event susceptible to weather, but which carried on regardless was The Big Jubilee Lunch.

Estimates put the numbers taking part across the country with their soggy sandwiches and rain diluted tea at 6 million.

The Queen's eldest child, Prince Charles, along with his second wife, Camilla, Duchess of Cornwall attended Piccadilly's gathering.

The flotilla and lunch formed the main events of the second day of celebrations. During the first, the Queen indulged her passion for horse racing by attending the Derby at Epsom.

More on her love for the sport later, but the event itself gave her an enjoyable start to the four days of celebrations.

Despite a decided nip in the air (Welsh Mezzo Soprano Kathryn Jenkins may have regretted her decision to wear a backless dress as she waited to perform the National Anthem), the course was packed.

The crowd waited in anticipation of both the season's major flat racing Classic and the opportunity of glimpsing Queen Elizabeth.

The Derby itself, though, proved not to be one of its finest races, with favourite Camelot easing to victory by a comfortable five lengths.

The highlight of day three of the Diamond Jubilee celebrations saw the Queen attend a concert in the Mall. Tickets were awarded by ballot, and those attending were treated to a picnic prior to the show.

Whilst the event itself went off smoothly, there was an insight into the pressures on a monarch when public and private priorities collide.

Prince Phillip became ill on the day with a bladder infection, and was hospitalized for the Monday evening concert. However, the Queen still managed to see some of the performances.

The concert featured many stars from the fields of music and comedy. Comedian Rob Brydon compered the event, with support from fellow comics including Jimmy Carr and Lee Mack.

Music was provided by the likes of Elton John, Cliff Richard and former Beatle Paul McCartney, who performed songs including 'Let it Be' and 'All My Loving.'

He led artists in a rousing finale of 'Ob La Di, Ob La Da' and, with the Queen now present; Prince Charles delivered a moving tribute to his parents.

The Queen's reluctance to abdicate and pass the Monarchy onto her eldest son is often the subject of debate and jokes, but during the speech there was a glimpse into the more private aspects of life within the Royal Family.

By referring to his sovereign as 'Mummy', and telling her that she made him 'proud to be British', he clearly touched a nerve, with his mother's normally reserved public face just wobbling for a second.

Dressed elegantly in gold, the Queen momentarily looked down, and was clearly seen to bite at her lower lip, before inclining her head and regaining her normal poise as she heard the personal epithet from her son.

A series of beacons were lit in her honour, including ones on the highest points of the four countries of the United Kingdom. The final beacon was lit by the Queen herself to signify the end of the concert.

Some moments seemed to capture the occasion perfectly. The pop group Madness bouncing on the roof of the palace as they performed their hit, 'Our House' and a magical extract from Michael Morpurgo's 'War Horse' performed by the

National Theatre. The play is known to be one of the Queen's favourites.

Tuesday June 5th, the final day of the celebrations, was more muted with a Service of Thanksgiving held at St Paul's Cathedral amongst the highlights.

The long weekend culminated as the Royal Family, minus a recovering Prince Phillip, gathered on the balcony of Buckingham Palace.

Both they and the enormous crowd watched an RAF fly past which included Spitfires, a Hurricane and Lancaster Bomber, as well as the Red Arrows.

It is hard to put a figure on the cost of the Diamond Jubilee celebrations. The treasury estimated £1.3 billion, although the overwhelming majority of this came from loss of industrial output resulting from the additional day of national holiday.

This figure has to be set against the pleasure millions derived from the weekend's events and the benefits the Royal Family bring to Britain's economy.

Not unlike the little ships that had combined to heroic effect on the shores of Dunkirk, so small stories from the weekend combined to make the occasion so special.

In Sheffield, a hotel put on a special celebratory tea for local couples who had reached their own Diamond Jubilees.

On crowded Chelsea Bridge, a policeman made sure that children could get to the front to see the flotilla pass.

And the lady herself? She expressed that she felt humbled by the attention paid to her. She expressed heartfelt thanks to the organisers and participants in the events.

As always with the Royals, it is difficult to see beyond the public face into the private world, but for those who saw her live or on TV over those four days, there were hints of the emotions she felt.

The strongest of those seemed to be pride. Pride in her family, in her achievements and in the response of her nation.

Annus Horribilis and Other Bleak Times

If 2012 marked one of the highlights of her reign, then 1992 provided the opposite.

This was a year in which nothing seemed to go right, a year in which three of her children separated or divorced, and in which her beloved Windsor Castle suffered a terrible fire.

It was also a year that marked, from some quarters at least, a threat to the nation's affection for the Royal Family.

The first bombshell came in the month following the Queen's Ruby Jubilee. On March 19th, the Palace announced that the Duke and Duchess of York (Prince Andrew and Sarah Ferguson) were to separate. They had been married for six years.

The couple, who have two daughters (Beatrice and Eugenie), remain friendly, and shared the same home for twenty years after their separation. They are still often seen together.

The demands of the Prince's naval career are thought to have been a trigger for the split. Having only spent forty days together in five years, the newly appointed Duchess wanted to be more than just a stay at home Royal.

The couple had known each other on and off since childhood. They shared a common interest in polo, although the sport had a negative effect on the young Sarah when her mother walked out on the family.

She left to be with Argentinian player Hector Barrantes. Her daughter was just twelve.

Perhaps the formality of the era, and the expectation to show a stiff upper lip, contributed to the breakdown of the marriage. Sarah discovered after just two weeks of matrimony that her new husband would be posted at sea.

She went through her first pregnancy with him away, and he received just ten days with his new daughter before once again returning to service.

Sarah was told just to get on with it and not to make a fuss.

Given that the couple's friendship has since endured so well, and the Duchess did remain mostly on good terms with the Royal family, the separation offers an insight into the challenge of being a modern Royal.

The conflict between the traditions of the monarchy and the way people now like to live their lives is hard.

Whilst people will hold differing views as to how far the perks of the position compensate for any lack of privacy and independence, but personal relationships need time and space to flourish.

Sarah Ferguson would feature yet again in the news that year when in August the Daily Mirror printed intimate pictures of her with a Texan businessman, John Bryan.

Looking back, the photos are extremely tame by current standards. But they represented the fact that becoming a Windsor meant every aspect of your life was open to scrutiny.

Having faced the announcement of the break-up of one of her children's marriages, the following month Princess Anne, Elizabeth's only daughter, announced that she and her husband, Captain Mark Phillips, had divorced.

The Princess had been the first of the Queen's children to marry, tying the knot at Westminster Abbey in 1973.

The pair had been separated for three years, and had two children. Peter and his sister, Zara, were the first grandchildren of the current reign.

Zara would go on to win silver for the United Kingdom at the London Olympics – the medal being presented by her mother.

The Princess was named Sports Personality of the Year in 1971, beating footballer George Best and Welsh Rugby legend Barry John to the award.

The following year, Phillips won Gold as a part of the Three Day Eventing team at the Munich Olympics.

However, despite (as with Prince Andrew and Sarah Ferguson) remaining friends, pressures on the marriage told.

A brief internet search for articles written around the time of their separation gives an insight into the way the Royal's previously untouchable status was being eroded.

Firstly, whilst Princess Anne received a reasonably smooth ride, her husband was lambasted for trapping his wife in an emotionally barren marriage.

Whilst there is little doubt that the couple grew apart during their fifteen year union, there is an absence of evidence published in support of the accusations.

Even the Queen herself comes under fire, accused of 'orchestrating' the separation and being behind the leak of secret letters between her daughter and the man she would marry later in the year.

The press seeks to create intrigue. Allegations of secret associations with a call girl, those caught up being forced into hiding and even, incredibly, a largely unsupported allegation that one of his children may have been fathered by somebody other than Mark Phillips.

It is hard to equate this treatment of the Royal Family with the adulation it received 20 years later.

Then. towards the end of the year, on 9th December, the Palace announced the separation of the dream couple, Prince Charles and Lady Diana Spencer.

Years of speculation had surrounded the couple and the state of their marriage. The previous month, the Queen had stated in a speech that 1992 had been her annus horribilis (terrible year).

Clearly, she would have been aware of the couple's problems even though they had not yet been revealed.

When Prime Minister John Major, winner of the year's earlier general election, announced that there were no plans for a divorce, and that the Princess might still become Queen, the news was treated with derision by the popular press.

Charles and Diana had seemed the perfect couple. Their wedding, in 1981, transfixed not only the nation, but the whole world.

An estimated three quarters of a billion people watched the service on television.

Diana won the heart of the country. She seemed to possess the perfect Princess's background and character.

The Spencer family lived in the aristocratic Althorp House in Northamptonshire. After her parents' divorce, she attended boarding schools in Norfolk and Kent.

But despite her privileged upbringing, so much about Diana struck a chord with people.

She was not the brightest student, but was a fine sports player, excelling in swimming, tennis and skiing.

Dance was also a passion and skill. Her ambition at a young age was to become a ballerina but even her failure to succeed here (she grew too tall) endeared her to folk.

Everybody has broken dreams – but not everybody grows up to marry a Prince.

As a schoolgirl, she developed a reputation for kindness to her fellows. A trait that she maintained through her too short life.

Like so many young people, she wanted to find her own way in the world and took a job after leaving school.

She began by cleaning and babysitting. She moved on to work with young children in a Kindergarten. Her favourite pudding was not some exotic fancy, but good old bread and butter pudding.

A perfect background for a 'people's princess'.

If the Royal Family could have designed a person to become Charles' wife and in doing so win the hearts of the nation, their creation would not have been very different to Lady Di.

The couple met when she was in her late teens. She had attended, for a brief period, a Swiss finishing school, and, at the time, the Prince was dating her elder sister, Lady Sarah Spencer.

They were engaged at nineteen, and married at twenty. The Prince was by this time under external pressure to marry, certainly from without and possibly from within his family.

Diana's grandmother was a former lady in waiting to the Queen Mother, and the two remained great friends. Many considered that they had encouraged the union, something both later denied.

The wedding was notable for many things – her dress; the glamour and pomp of the occasion; the unbelievable crowds and TV audiences.

It was also notable for something that wasn't there.

In her vows, Diana chose to exclude the requirement to 'obey' her husband.

Whilst this vow is often omitted these days, with both partners recognizing that obedience is not a healthy trait in a loving relationship, in the early 80s it was normally retained.

To have it omitted from a service involving as traditional an institution as the Royal Family was astonishing.

It was an indication that this was a lady who would see her role as a royal differently to those of the older generations.

Although the marriage appeared to be perfect, there were problems from the outset.   Prince Charles would later call the union a 'Greek Tragedy.'

In an interview with journalist Martin Bashir, during a ground breaking television documentary, Diana told the nation that there were always three in their marriage (the third being Charles' future wife and long time love, Camilla Parker Bowles).

'It was a bit crowded,' she admitted.

Charles' relationship with the future Duchess of Cornwall had been kept as quiet as possible. She was married, and ostensibly her presence at many of the couple's engagements was as that of a friend and mentor to the younger woman.

Marriage for Charles and Camilla would have been difficult. She would have needed to divorce, and at the time to marry a divorcee would remove any chance of the gaining the throne.

The Queen's uncle, King Edward, had been forced to abdicate in order to marry his love, Wallis Simpson.

But the continued affections between the old friends created a highly unstable start to the royal marriage.

Like so many spouses of royals before, Diana also found the open window on her life unbearable. Increasingly, the press sought negative stories about the House of Windsor as the hard edged, money driven 80s progressed.

In a speech during 1993, the Princess revealed the true turmoil of living under constant media scrutiny.

Whilst admitting that she knew that the press would invade her public and, to a lesser extent, private life, she confessed that she had not been aware of the extent of the invasion.

'It has been hard to bear.' She concluded, with typical Royal understatement.

One of the personal stories that the press would not let go surrounded her alleged eating disorder, bulimia.

The condition affects people by making them restrict the amount of food they consume, then binge eat later. After this, they will make themselves sick, or use laxatives to expel the meal from their body.

Today, we are learning more about this mental health condition. But back in the late 1980s and early 1990s, the condition was one that was considered 'weird', and therefore newsworthy.

Especially when it involved a princess.

Diana revealed the extent pressures on her to be a perfect wife and royal. But, even princesses are normal people, with strengths and flaws, with ambitions and weaknesses.

But, as a royal 30 years ago, those normal, negative traits had to be suppressed.

Yet through all the tribulations, all the exposure, Diana retained the warmth of the public. Her smile, looks and, especially, the random acts of kindness proffered helped people to understand that she was a real person.

In his book 'Notes from a Small Island' American writer Bill Bryson recalls walking through Windsor Great Park. He moves aside as a large car approaches and is warmed and heartened by the glorious, genuine smile the driver, Lady Di, awards him.

With the Aids epidemic seeming to run out of control, and ill informed rumour spreading about how it is contracted, the Princess helped to change public perception of the disease.

By visiting patients, and shaking their hands without any form of glove or covering, she sent the message that Aids could not be caught by simple contact.

She told the public that these poor people needed hugs and support, adding 'Having HIV does not make people dangerous to know.'

Her message of tolerance and understanding was echoed recently by her son, Prince Harry, when he advised against complacency towards the disease.

Perhaps, more than anything else, it was her relationship with William and Harry that cemented the adoration of the public.

Rather than send them far away to school, as had happened with their father (he had attended firstly

Cheam School near Newbury, then Gordonstoun, in the north of Scotland), the young princes would attend schools much closer to their home.

Once old enough, they attended Ludgrove School, in Wokingham, before moving to nearby Eton College.

Although both are boarding schools, Princess Di stayed in constant touch. She was frequently to be observed attending school matches, sitting quietly under a tree as might any other parent.

Her love for her boys was absolute, her determination to protect them from the scrutiny she had endured paramount.

Her belief that they should grow up as normally as possible, forgoing many royal traditions and expectations, won her both support from the public and displeasure from within the royal household.

And it was her death speeding through a Parisian underpass, the paparazzi in close pursuit, at the desperately young age of 36, that began the process of returning the Queen and her family to the much loved institution we saw during the early years of her reign.

Who can forget the image of Diana's young sons parading behind her coffin, their father, grandfather and maternal uncle with them?

Or the desperately poignant 'Mummy' spelled out in flowers on her coffin?

Today, in 2017, her sons have just begun to talk publicly about the loss of their mother, how it affected them and how they coped (or didn't). It is a measure of how far the family has come that they are able to do this.

But back in 1992, one further event was to besmirch the Queen's year.

On 20th November, millions of pounds worth of damage was caused when fire broke out at Windsor Castle.

The 900 year old building was undergoing renovations when, just before midday, the fire broke out.

It is thought that a spot light was left too close to an alter curtain in the Queen's private chapel. The fire spread quickly to neighbouring rooms and private apartments, with workers in the building rushing to remove priceless antiques before they were destroyed.

Assisting in the evacuation was Prince Andrew. He was engulfed in smoke as he sought to save the antiquities.

St George's Hall suffered most damage in the fire, and its roof collapsed. However, with most antiques and paintings removed for the restorations, just a handful suffered damage.

The only painting to be lost had an interesting history. 'George III and the Prince of Wales Reviewing Troops' by Sir William Beechey, showed the King on horseback, with his sons and other generals.

The 1798 painting caused controversy at the time. It was created during a period of unrest between the King and his Prince.

When he discovered that the artist had included the Prince of Wales in the picture, apparently at the bidding of the his wife, George was outraged and ordered that the painting be burned.

His orders were disobeyed, and when the King and his son resolved their differences, the painting gained favour.

Would that the King had known that nearly 300 years later, his wish would come to saddening fruition.

After the fire, damage from which took years to repair, the Queen was seen sadly moving between parts of the damaged building. The rain on the day seeming to reflect her dampened spirits.

Repairs cost £36.5 million. They were met in parts by charges made to tour the castle, the opening of Buckingham palace to tourists, the Queen's own money, an appeal and public funds.

It was as a result of the fire that the Queen took the decision to begin paying tax on her income.

The year ended on a better note for the Queen, with the marriage of Princess Anne to Timothy Laurence, but all in all it had been a terrible year.

Partial destruction of her beloved Windsor Castle, and further damage to her family through the break up of three of her children's marriages.

All of this lapped up and slavered over by a press keen to extract every detail from the stories.

It was truly the Queen's annus horribilis, and things would have to get better.

Prince Phillip – her 'Strength and Stay'

One of the rocks that supports the Queen during her lowest moments is her husband, the Duke of Edinburgh

Phillip Mountbatten was born in 1921 on the island of Corfu and into the Royal families of Greece and Denmark.

His early years lacked stability – his father fell into exile and his mother frequently required treatment for schizophrenia.

His education took place in France and Germany, as well as the United Kingdom.

In a journey his son would later follow, he attended Cheam Preparatory School and, later, Gordonstoun.

He was one of the first pupils at the Scottish School, which had been founded when the Jewish owner of the Prince's German School fled persecution from the Nazis. During the war, he served in the Royal Navy.

As the young Elizabeth's 3rd cousin on her paternal side, and second cousin once removed on the other, he met his future wife for first time in 1934, when they were both still children.

Their relationship grew, and after the war he became a British citizen, adopting the name Mountbatten from his maternal grandparents. After receiving permission to ask for her hand in marriage, the two were wed in 1947.

However, such were the continuing tensions following the war that Phillip's sisters, who had married German aristocrats, were not permitted to be invited to the wedding.

The Prince, now Duke of Edinburgh, continued on active service until his wife's coronation in 1952.

With the accession of Elizabeth to the throne, a thorny issue arose. What to call the Royal House?

As is the case today, the wife typically takes her husband's surname upon marriage - even if she is a queen - and so the House of Mountbatten would have been the logical choice.

Unsurprisingly, this was advocated by Phillip's Uncle, Earl Louis Mountbatten. However, Winston Churchill did not support his war time military leader, blaming him for losing India.

Churchill, supported by Elizabeth's grandmother, Queen Mary, favoured the retention of the existing name, Windsor.

His view prevailed, and a decree was issued. In a prelude to a career of speaking his mind, Phillip said it as he saw it, describing himself as no more than an amoeba attached to the great rock of the monarchy.

'I am the only man in the country not allowed to give his name to his own children,' said the man whose wife would later call him her 'strength and stable'.

The whole incident seems to be another example of the institution doing things their way, out of line with how the remainder of the country works.

The Duke is patron of numerous organisations. Although his work is now slowing down, he is unrelenting in his support of the Queen and in the performance of his public duties.

However, another side of Prince Phillip came to light in the immediate aftermath of the death of Princess Diana.

At the time, most of the family, including the two young princes, were staying in their home at Balmoral, Scotland.

Philip and the Queen kept the children at Balmoral for five days, allowing them to grieve out of sight of the prying eyes of the press.

They received enormous criticism for this, with the public, often voiced by the media, slating them for not showing their feelings in the open.

Their self-imposed seclusion caused dismay and outrage, and only later, in the cold light of reality, could the sense of these actions be understood.

Who knows what advice they received, but on this rare occasion the interests of their family were, rightly, made the priority.

When Diana's sons, inevitably overwhelmed by the monumental funeral, hesitated to walk behind the coffin, Philip stepped in

'If I walk, will you walk with me?' asked the Prince, just like any other grandfather supporting their youngsters would do.

If Philip, however, is known for anything, it is for making the sort of comments of which headline writers and stand-up comedians dream.

As much as we can view them now with warm nostalgia, some of his utterances could have caused offence, and probably did.

'How do you keep them off the booze long enough to get them through the test?' he once asked a Scottish driving instructor.

'It looks as though it was put in by an Indian,' he commented, pointing out an old-fashioned fuse box in Edinburgh.

'You're a woman, aren't you?' he queried of a lady Nigerian when she passed him a gift in 1984.

But if these comments were, at the very least, extremely close to the mark in their absolute political incorrectness, others have been much easier to digest.

And smile at.

'Yak, yak, yak!' he called to his wife as she delayed entry onto the Royal Yacht Britannia to talk to some well-wishers.

'I wish he'd turn the microphone off,' about singer Elton John, and 'Do you gargle with pebbles?' to the power-voiced Tom Jones.'

'Are you asking if the Queen is going to die?' he snapped when questioned about when Charles would ascend to the throne.

He remarked on his 90th birthday that 'Bits were beginning to drop off,' and in the Autumn of 2017 he will retire fully from public life.

But he will do so with the memory of being at the Queen's side during some of her greatest and most challenging moments.

2002 might in some ways have been another annus horribilus, the year in which both her sister, Margaret, and her mother passed away.

The Queen Mother had seemed indestructible, and that trait was passed to the Queen as, with Philip inevitably at her side, she fought on through her personal grief to ensure that public enjoyed her Golden Jubilee.

In 1979, they stood together in the aftermath of the murder of Lord Mountbatten, the Queen's cousin, at the hands of the IRA.

Then in 2012, in celebration of the on-going peace process, the couple met politician and former IRA commander Martin McGuiness and Sinn Fein leader Gerry Adams.

A Passion for Horses

If, like the majority of people, the Queen's greatest love is for her spouse and family, then high up in the chasing pack is her passion for all things equine, and in particular, horse racing.

Following her first riding lesson, at just three years old, her Grandfather, King George V, gave Elizabeth and her sister Margaret a special gift.

A Shetland pony called Peggy.

Her love of horse racing began in earnest after WWII. Upon ascending to the throne in 1952 she inherited the royal racing colours.

The famous purple with gold braid and scarlett sleeves, topped with a gold fringed black cap, have many times been first past the post.

She had her debut winner in May 1952 when Choir Boy crossed the line in the Wilburton

Handicap at Newmarket. Better was soon to follow.

For anybody who lives in, or who tries to pass through the Berkshire town of Ascot in late June, the name Royal Ascot will evoke mixed reactions.

Locals erect scarecrow like figures in their front gardens, miniature jockeys and the like. Everybody within a ten mile radius prepares their day to avoid being on the road after the final race.

Thousands upon thousands of race-goers descend on the town for the five days of the Festival, dressed up in their best finery.

Hotel prices go through the roof as proprietors cash in on the meeting and roads suffer the sort of congestion associated with London's North Circular during the rush hour.

Ascot racecourse was founded in 1711 by Queen Anne, and has enjoyed the patronage of eleven subsequent monarchs. For our current Queen, however, attendance is more of a joy than a duty.

Each day begins with the Royal Procession, in which the Queen, along with other members of the Royal Family in attendance, travel in carriages along the track.

The Queen herself is a breeder and owner of many thoroughbred horses, and has had a number of winners at Ascot.

Indeed, in 2013 she became the first Monarch to own the winning horse in Ascot's premier race, the Gold Cup.

Her filly, Estimate, triumphed in a close finish. A quick internet search throws up links to find videos of the event.

There is something heart warming about seeing the Queen, usually so proper, letting herself go. With an enormous smile splitting her face, she is seen shouting encouragement, slapping her seat in excitement.

These are rare glimpses into the personal side of the Queen.

Estimate achieved a hat trick of Ascot wins and was still going strong in 2017. Other horses, though, have also achieved great things for the monarch.

Some experts, including Sir Michael Oswald (the Queen Mother's racing manager) concluded that the best horse the Queen ever owned was Dunfermline.

Although the horse did not shine as a two year old, the following year she went on, under the training of Major Dick Hern, to win two of the racing calendar's Classics, the Oaks and the St Leger.

This was in 1977, and provided a fitting tribute to her Silver Jubilee.

Unfortunately, a decade later, the relationship between the Queen and her trainer was severely damaged.

The story goes that, following heart trouble, Dick Hern lay seriously ill in hospital. Doctors were divided as to whether his health would be sufficiently regained to allow him to train again.

The Earl of Carnarvon, the Queen's racing manager, decided to fire Hern from his role as trainer of some of the Queen's horses.

He made the decision based, he says, on the advice of the jockey club's medical expert, ignoring the guidance from other doctors treating Hern.

This had the added impact of meaning that the trainer and his wife would need to leave their home in Berkshire. The property, attached to the stables, belonged to the Queen at that time.

What particularly annoyed Hern was that the message was relayed via his wife, rather than in person to himself.

Although subsequently the couple were granted residence in another property, the harm had been done, and the racing community gathered in support around the trainer.

This happened in 1988, when feelings towards the Royal Family where heading towards their lowest ebb, and was yet another example of the House of Windsor, and its employees, handling sensitive matters in a way that left them open to criticism.

Three years prior to Dunfermline's Classic successes, another of the Queen's horses, Highclere, achieved an impressive double.

She was victorious in the 1000 guineas and the French Oaks, a race that for once, the Queen's busy official schedule allowed her to attend.

The Queen's horses have racked up well over 1600 wins between them, including every Classic except The Derby.

The appropriately named Pall Mall won the 2000 guineas in 1958. Following a disappointing start to the season, the horse fell in the betting stakes to become a 20-1 outsider by the start of the race.

Taking the lead a furlong and a half out, the particularly handsome chestnut held on to win by half a length. Sadly, the Queen missed the race through illness.

Cousin to the Queen, Margaret Rhodes, offered a perspective on the Monarch's love of horse racing.

She explained that taking up the throne meant a lot of normal emotions and ambitions would have to be kept down, hidden away from a world that scrutinized her so closely.

But her cousin's love of horses was different. This passion gave her a chance to be a normal person, with normal enthusiasms.

In one of her favourite pieces of literature, War Horse, Michael Morpurgo tells of the horrors of the first World War. He does it through the vehicle of an equine narrator, Joey.

Because Joey is a horse, people are open and truthful around him – after all, he is not a human, he won't judge or complain.

Perhaps this is a little how the Queen feels, that to her horses she is not a queen, just another human being.

That must be a huge relief.

Queen Elizabeth II

Elizabeth Alexandra Mary was born into the House of Windsor at 2.40am on April 21st, 1926. She was delivered by Caesarian section.

Had she been born a decade earlier, it would have been into the House of Saxe-Coburg-Gotha.

However, anti-German feeling during the First World War encouraged George V to change the family's name to Windsor.

Along with her younger sister, Elizabeth was home educated, with many of the lessons being delivered by their much loved governess, Marion Crawford, or Crawfie as she became known.

The governess committed fully to the royal girls, even setting up a guides' pack so they could mix with children of their own age.

She had been hand selected by the Queen Mother and seemed to display a similar indifference to academic matters as the royal household itself.

Instead, Crawfie ensured, as far as was possible (which was not especially far) that her charges experienced some touches of everyday life, the sort other girls of their age would see.

This included a ride on the London Underground, and a trip to London Zoo.

When the girls became adults, Crawfie remained a confidant. Now married, with a small pension but a grace and favour cottage, she stayed close to the girls.

Elizabeth and Margaret were regular visitors to their old governess.

On one occasion, the newly wed Elizabeth turned up unannounced at the cottage, with Philip in tow. Whilst Crawfie hastily put on a pot of tea, Philip repaired the house's dodgy boiler.

But matters turned sour when the former governess was persuaded to write a book about her time with the royal princesses, which was serialized in the American press.

She was forced to leave her cottage, and all links to the family were cut. Within royal parlance, the phrase 'doing a Crawfie' came to mean exploiting the family for financial gain.

Crawfie died, widowed and lonely, in an Aberdeenshire nursing home in 1988.

The 78 year-old had succumbed to cancer. In a moving twist, she instructed her solicitor to send to the Queen a boxful of personal photos, letters and mementoes. These are stored in the royal archives.

In her book, which by modern standards can only be viewed as a fond portrayal of her charges, Crawfie identified the young Elizabeth as diligent and orderly.

Winston Churchill recalled that she had a mind of her own, but was very sensible. Both identified her sense of duty, which would stay with her right up to the present time.

Elizabeth's birth had prompted only moderate public interest because, as third in the line to the throne, she was not expected to become Queen.

Her uncle, Edward, the Prince of Wales, was first in line and any children he produced would overtake her in the order of succession.

After her grandfather's death in 1936, Edward did indeed take over the throne.

But his abdication over the constitutional crisis created by his decision to marry a divorced woman, Wallis Simpson, changed things dramatically.

Suddenly, her father was King and Elizabeth was heir presumptive. Had her parents given birth to a son, he would have become heir apparent, above her in the order of succession.

Both Elizabeth and Margaret spent most of the war living in Windsor Castle, just a short distance from London which, of course, underwent enormous and catastrophic bombing.

Elizabeth's first radio broadcast was made aged 14 in 1940, and was addressed to evacuated children. Later, in 1943 she made her first official solo appearance, visiting the Grenadier guards.

Towards the end of the war, she joined the Women's Auxilliary Territorial Service, gaining the service number 230873. She attained the rank of honorary Junior Commander.

On VE day, the princesses anonymously joined crowds celebrating in the streets, and Elizabeth recalled being swept away with the joy of the occasion and the celebrating public.

The girls expressed a fear of being recognized. Somebody, somewhere that day unknowingly (or perhaps otherwise) joined arms, dancing and singing, with their future Queen.

On her first overseas engagement, made to southern Africa with her parents when she was 21, she pledged to serve and devote herself to the people of the Commonwealth.

Would she have imagined that she would still be honoring this promise 70 years later.

As was mentioned in a previous chapter, her husband's sisters were not invited to her wedding.

Such was the power of tradition and established propriety that neither was her uncle, the former King.

A small story from her wedding is that, because the country was still recovering from the impact of war (it was only two years since VE day), she had to save up her ration cards to get enough material for her dress.

Charles, the Queen's first child, was born in November 1948, with her only daughter, Anne, following in 1950.

Her father's health declined badly during the following year, and the young wife and mother frequently stepped in for him on official occasions.

In 1952, Elizabeth and Philip undertook a tour of Australia and New Zealand, via Kenya. Her Private Secretary, perhaps sensing that the King may not have long to live, carried a Declaration of Accession on the trip.

And on 6th February, her husband announced to his wife that she had become Queen of all her Realms.

The couple returned quickly to England, and took up residence in Buckingham Palace.

In keeping with protocol, we can garner little of the emotional state of the Queen at that time. Her father had just died, her Grandmother would not survive until the Coronation.

Her sister was seeking to marry a divorcee sixteen years her senior. Such an action would be severely frowned upon.

And, at just 25 years of age, she had become head of the largest Empire in the world.

All this, at a time of dramatic social and political change, not least within an Empire that was transforming into a Commonwealth of Nations, with all that this implied.

The Empire's children were growing up and, though still part of the family, were spreading their wings.

In such a state of post war turmoil, the best conclusions that can be made are drawn from the facts that are known.

The coronation was an enormous success. It was the first event of its kind to be televised, and was watched by, for then, an enormous audience.

Later that year, the royal couple toured the world, visiting 13 countries and covering 40000 miles, travelling by air, land and sea.

Wherever they went, they were greeted with adulation from the public.

The date of the coronation itself was selected in part because it was predicted to be a dry day. In true weather forecasting fashion, Tuesday, June 2nd 1953 turned out to be wet!

Hard to imagine now, but political figures were very much against the live broadcast of the event on television. It was the Queen herself who finally made the decision that would lead to an enormous boost for the television industry.

In addition to the 27 million viewers who found a set, a further 11 million are believed to have listened in on the radio.

2000 journalists and 500 photographers lined the route to Westminster Abbey including a future first lady – Jackie Kennedy (then Bouvier) worked for the Washington Times-Herald.

Such were the worldwide celebrations that the traditional British street party was adopted in New York.

One person not celebrating was Princess Anne, who was deemed too young to attend. Sibling rivalry must have entered overdrive when she discovered that her brother would be permitted to go.

He became the first heir to the throne to attend his own mother's coronation. However, the three hour service may have been somewhat long even for a doting son.

The event was organized by the 16th Duke of Norfolk, who would later plan the funeral of Winston Churchill. Apparently, the only glitch during the event was that at one point the Queen forgot to curtsey.

But she had practiced well, using curtains as robes and maids as important dignitaries, whilst awaiting the big day at Buckingham Palace.

After the event, guests were served an original dish which has now become a common part of summer picnics and salads.

Coronation Chicken was created for the occasion, not least because it could be prepared in advance.

To complete a perfect day, weather apart, news came in that, a few day's earlier, Everest had been conquered.

4606 miles away, give or take one or two vertical rather than horizontal units, Edmund Hillary and Sherpa Tensing Norgay reached the summit of the Himalayan peak.

During her long reign, the Queen would go on to have two more children. Andrew, born in 1960 and Edward who entered the world in 1964.

She has eight grandchildren and five great grandchildren.

Current heirs to the throne are firstly Prince Charles, then Prince William followed by his children Prince George and Princess Charlotte.

Until 2015, had Prince William produced another son, then the boy would have overtaken Charlotte in order or succession, but following a decision in 2011, the law changed to one that did not place male heirs above their female siblings.

A Lifetime of Service

Undoubtedly, one of the greatest strengths of Queen Elizabeth II has been her commitment to the performance of her official duties.

There are significant differences between her constitutional powers, her real powers, her official duties and her rights.

Although in theory (but not in practice) she could, in no particular order, conduct a war with Brittany, make peace with Cornwall (maybe if the rest of the country remains at war with the County, then that explains Cornish pasties).

She could sack the Army, make everybody a peer of the realm and pardon every prisoner in the country.

In reality she has only three effective royal rights, and they do not amount to anything especially significant. She has right to be consulted, to encourage and to warn.

Rather like her rights, her powers are largely honorary. She opens and dissolves Parliament, appoints and dismisses Prime Ministers – but only by tradition. She cannot act upon a whim.

And whilst she does not need a postage stamp, and can ride along Rotten Row in a carriage (the rest of the world should walk) these are not of any importance beyond the traditional.

Because we have a constitutional monarchy, the actual duties of the Queen, in which she is supported by her family, are wide ranging but hard to specify.

As Head of State, she undertakes representational and constitutional duties which have evolved over the last millennium. For example, she will host World leaders when they visit the United Kingdom.

Over time, she has accommodated President Bashar Al-Assad, the Syrian leader, and Zimbabwe's dictator Robert Mugabe.

Assad is accused of murdering millions of his own subjects in the continuing hostilities in the region.

Mugabe was awarded an honorary knighthood by the Queen, but had it stripped in 1997 because of the nature of his regime and his treatment of opponents.

In 1973, the President of Zaire was invited and represented as an important ally against the influence of the Soviet Union. In reality, he was an embezzler and murderous dictator.

Later in the '70s, Romanian leader Nicolae Ceausescu came to the Palace, in the mistaken belief that he could be encouraged to embrace a pro West approach.

The misguidedness of the act was emphasized a decade later when he was overthrown and summarily executed by his own people.

It is, of course, not the Queen herself who offers such invitations, that pleasure falls to politicians, but she is the one who has to meet with them, share a carriage with them, and invite them into her home.

If these responsibilities as Head of State are prescribed, her duties as Head of the Nation, and Head of the Commonwealth are much more nebulous.

However, certain traditional titles remain. The Head of State is also the Head of the Armed Forces, the Head of the Church of England and she holds governmental duties.

All documents and government reports are delivered to the Queen. She also hosts at least three Garden Parties (with around 8000 guests each time) every year.

And, of course, she visits numerous hospitals, schools, factories, openings and more every year.

In these duties, she acts as a figurehead, a symbol of unity.

In practical terms creating such unity involves certain specific duties, such as laying a wreath at the Cenotaph each year and delivering the annual Christmas message.

But being monarch in the twenty first century involves many more general, fluctuating responsibilities.

During conditions of War, she has been a figurehead for national togetherness. At times of crisis, such as in recent terrorist attacks, her (and her family's) visits to terror sites, hospitals and communities helps to bring differing factions of society together.

The Queen has been monarch to thirteen Prime Ministers. Winston Churchill was the incumbent when she acceded to the throne.

Her relationships with them has been varied. Although complete discretion is supposedly assured in discussions between the heads of

Parliament and State some interesting truths have leaked out.

Many believe her first Prime Minister was also her favourite, their meetings often punctuated with peals of laughter.

Members of the Household reported that Churchill often left the Palace with tears in his eyes. We presume of joy.

Years later, the Queen herself said that he had been her favourite Premier, being such fun.

She was fond of all her early Prime Ministers; perhaps the fact that she was so much younger than them helped with their nervousness.

Labour leader Harold Wilson, who served two separate spells at Number 10, was another she particularly liked.

Whilst that Prime Minister came across as a down to earth person who was in touch with the electorate, he also taught her a lot about politics.

Less is known about her relationship with the Conservative Edward Heath. Although, the fact the he fell asleep at a dinner hosted by the Queen, admittedly many years later, could be telling.

She spotted the indiscretion, along with John Major, but they decided not to mention it and, when he finally awoke, it was as if nothing had happened.

James Callaghan earned the rare honour of having a flower placed in his button hole by Her Majesty's hand. But her relationship with the first female Premier, Margaret Thatcher, did not seem to gel as easily.

Not one for the pomp and tradition of the Royal Family, in addition the Grantham lass did not like Balmoral, and it seemed as though the relationship with the Queen was at times strained.

The same could be said regarding Tony Blair. His sense that he had saved the family from public opinion over the death of Diana did not endear him to the monarch.

However, between those two long serving Prime Ministers another homely, down to earth Premier established a warm relationship.

John Major would often enjoy informal meals with the Queen and Prince Philip, taking along his wife, Nora, on many occasions.

He was also the first Prime Minister to be younger than the monarch.

Only two former Premiers were not invited to Prince William's wedding. Tony Blair and Gordon Brown.

Moving on, both David Cameron and Theresa May have re-established warm relations between the Palace and Number 10.

The Queen and other members of the Royal Family are patrons of over 3000 charities and organisations.

Such patronage gives prominence and publicity to the beneficiaries. More requests are made annually than can be accepted.

However, the Queen heads charities both great and small, from the Mothers' Union to the Red Cross.

After her 90th birthday, she began the process of passing on her charitable responsibilities to other members of the Royal family.

These included the children's organisations Bernardo's and the NSPCC, sporting institutions such as the Rugby Union and the Sport and Recreation Alliance, and charities supporting animals, for example, the Animal Health trust.

Amongst the other duties of the Queen is to reflect the excitement of the nation when extra special events take place.

The London Olympics was one such event, and the Nation was united in support and appreciation of her contribution to the opening ceremony.

Whilst there are rumours that it was not actually Her Majesty who sky dived into the arena, accompanied by James Bond, we can't be sure. Can we?

Nevertheless, she surprised us all by appearing in the now famous short film alongside Bond actor Daniel Craig.

Delivering her line – 'Good Evening Mr Bond' with perfect archness, and appearing beside her own Corgis, she delighted the watching world.

Later, she officially opened the games, but the film parody is what the public took away from Danny Boyle's innovative opening ceremony.

It is a sign of how far the monarchy has modernized since the dark days of the 80s and 90s that it was happily seen to laugh at itself.

Perhaps also a sign that the real Queen, viewed in private by her family and trusted friends, but not often when 'on duty', was being given a rare public outing.

So how does the Queen manage to fit in all her official duties, her visits and meetings, her family commitments and still enjoy time with her animals?

Whilst she is necessarily easing up as she moves into her 90s, she remains very busy. To gain a further insight, a typical day from a couple of years ago, when she was working at full speed, is offered below. She continues with many of the activities today.

Normally, having risen a little after eight, and been greeted by the playing of bagpipes (in no way one of the downsides of royalty), she will bathe then breakfast quietly.

Cornflakes or Special K with fruit are typical fare. Whilst we might imagine sumptuous meals, these are generally saved for special occasions.

For example, the Queen enjoys smoked salmon and her own farm eggs for breakfast at Christmas.

A reading of the papers follows, before moving on to the mail.

Receiving around 300 letters a day, she will select a few and pass the remainder on to a Lady in Waiting for her to respond.

Work then becomes harder as she deals with the Government red boxes, which contain all the official information from Parliament for her to peruse.

These are sent on every day of the year, excepting Christmas Day.

The Queen would previously often have spent the remainder of the morning on visits, frequently with Prince Phillip.

Use of the Royal Helicopter and RAF flights speeded up the travel times, allowing her to fit in more visits and meet more people, with the royal train used then, and now, on occasion.

Often, the train returns late at night or in the early hours, with the royals sleeping on board.

When not out on official duties, the Queen will spend the later part morning in meetings with a range of officials from all aspects of her work.

Meetings are kept short and focused, and will involve the likes of ambassadors and senior military figures.

Lunch is light and often taken alone, with fish and vegetables being a popular choice.

Formal lunches are held monthly for a variety of purposes and guests, such as people from the world of business, charity workers and occasionally to honour, for example, a retiring official.

With enormous demand on her to visit schools, openings, hospitals and suchlike, she will often (although less frequently these days) spend the afternoon on the road before arriving back for a quiet dinner in the early evening.

In the past, the Queen would frequently be away for periods overseas, but much of this work is now done by other royals, out of consideration for her age.

When not 'doing the rounds', the Queen, as romantic ideas suggest, takes afternoon tea – small old-fashioned penny sized jam sandwiches being a particular favourite.

Meetings with the Prime Minister are held weekly at 6.30 on a Wednesday. These are minute free occasions, with the subject matter remaining behind closed doors.

If the schedule allows, dinner will follow at around 7.30, following a measure of the Queen's favourite tipple, gin and dubonnet.

Later, the Palace will regularly host official parties, banquets and dinners.

Despite this busy daily schedule, when time allows, relaxation from the never ending round of official duties can take a number of forms.

Walking with her dogs, tending her corgis, spending time with, or finding out about, her horses are favourite past times.

Walking in Windsor Great Park is another treasured activity.

There is a well known story about such an occasion. The Queen is strolling through the Park accompanied by her security officer when a friendly American tourist sees them.

The American greets them enthusiastically, then drops her voice to ask conspiratorially, 'Hey, have you seen the Queen?'

'I haven't' replies Her Majesty, and then, pointing towards the Security Officer, states: 'But he has!'

Another popular form of relaxation is, as is the case for many, sitting in front of the TV. A sky box lurks in her apartment, and favourites are said to include dramas such as Downton Abbey.

Old comedies like Dad's Army and Last of the Summer Wine are popular, as are some soaps.

And so, it is reported, is the X Factor. Britain's Got Talent doesn't get a mention, but the enthusiasm contestants display for getting a spot at the Royal Variety Performance suggest that perhaps it should.

The Queen will still often work into the night, finishing off her red boxes and reviewing the parliamentary activities of the day.

She, along with many others of the royal family, receives a substantial income each year.

This is certainly more than offset by the contribution made to the economy through, for example, tourism.

It is further earned through the pleasure brought to millions – sports stars, actors, entertainers can earn substantial incomes but touch the hearts or liven the spirits of far fewer people.

But even without these benefits, many would argue that every penny the Queen receives, she certainly earns.

A Much Loved Monarch

There have been some awful monarchs in British history.

How about one who, according to Historian Robert Wilton, psychologically 'barely made it out of infancy, let alone adolescence, and ruled with little more policy than petulant self-gratification.'

That was Henry VII - wife murdering, religion destroying despot. Depending, of course, on your point of view.

Edward VIII comes out poorly in a review of historical writers, although others might argue that he was somebody who put love before monarchy, and it was more the prevailing times that were misguided.

Queen Elizabeth II, however, is up there with the best royal ruler of any era.

Whilst longevity inevitably contributes to our warmth for the Queen, there is more to her enduring popularity than this.

People will go to enormous lengths to show their appreciation of her. A home economics teacher from Scotland has amassed a collection of 10000 photos of the Queen.

The teacher attends so many royal events, that she is now recognized by the Monarch, who twice stopped her Range Rover to chat.

Imagine being out doing your shopping when Her Majesty pulls over and winds down the window.

In addition to her photos, the super fan has a collection of memorabilia that includes 400 mugs and 60 plates, as well as numerous books.

A town crier got himself in the news by, in best 'criering' mode, wishing the Queen a happy ninetieth birthday. Another man, aged 80, was prepared to sleep rough to guarantee a view of the monarch on her special day.

Followers dress in Union Jack tops, suits and jackets. Rosettes, commercial and home made, adorn fans and t shirt sellers do a roaring trade whenever the Queen makes a public appearance.

So, why does she create such intense feelings in people? The most common answer seems to be that there is an overwhelming wish to pay tribute to the Queen for her ongoing hard work.

Margaret Tyler, from Wembley, could claim to be the biggest royal fan of all. Amongst her collection of novelties is a solar powered Queen.

With four rooms of her house filled with memorabilia, her collection has an estimated value of £40000.

Margaret has met the Queen on four occasions, and gave her a cake for her 80th birthday.

Across the country, support for the monarchy has remained pretty constant at around 75%. Even during the dark years, the figure did not especially vary.

With a general skepticism towards many other institutions – the Government, the police and the media, for example, an institution that is ripe for mockery remains extremely popular.

After all, that institution is amongst the most closed and privileged imaginable. Yet, it remains deeply loved and respected.

Looking back to the coronation, the occasion was planned to be full of pomp and extravagance…at a point where bomb damage could be found in many corners of the capital.

A time of austerity existed, with food rationing still in place. Given that the war had led to a rapid change in society, where values were constantly being re evaluated, such an extravaganza as the coronation could have evoked angry reactions.

Given that the war leader, Winston Churchill, had been thrown out of power, and just as surprisingly pushed back in, to make the coronation such a flamboyant occasion was an enormous risk.

Little could have been more calculated to reinforce a sense of the haves, and have nots. Yet, the public, across all social strata, loved it.

Perhaps, despite all the change taking place, the coronation was somehow reassuring, a sign that Britain could do something special like nowhere else.

A reassurance that things could return to how they used to be. Not that many wanted that, but perhaps change was more welcome in the shadow of the security the slow moving monarchy provided.

Maybe this too is why, with the institution seeming completely out of touch with the rest of society in the 1980s, lambasted by the press but defiantly retaining its sense of 'knowing how to do things', people remained supportive.

We were prepared to criticize, but only in the certainty that little would change.

And perhaps that is why a monarch with 60 years on the throne during a time of the most rapid change in the country's history should remain so overwhelmingly popular.

Plus, of course, that the lady deserves such respect.

But…twenty per cent of the nation do not want a royal family. In parts of the country, Republicanism is strong. Even more so, in the Commonwealth, there has been significant opposition to the Queen in some places.

Republicanism in the United Kingdom is complex. In Ireland, it relates more to the removal of all British involvement in the running of the country, rather than just the abolition of the monarchy.

Nationalism in Wales and Scotland revolves around a wish for self Government more than the removal of the Queen.

Indeed, the main political parties for devolution, Plaid Cymru in Wales and the SNP in Scotland each support the idea that there would be a monarch as Head of State.

The extent to which this a genuinely held belief, or political pragmatism, is harder to judge.

The country has flirted with change. Under Cromwell in the seventeenth century, it was briefly a Republic.

In 1923 resolutions were proposed at the Labour Party's annual conference to move the UK towards a republican agenda, but they made little impact.

The main movement today seeking to abolish the monarchy in the United Kingdom is an organisation called Republic. It does not make it easy to find its membership numbers.

Instead, it claims to represent 12 million British Republicans. The protest group staged a demonstration at the Diamond Jubilee celebrations. They were joined by sympathizers from overseas.

The Guardian described their numbers in terms of 'dozens', and the protest angered many attendees looking forward to seeing the 1000 ship flotilla on the Thames.

The Commonwealth too now seems fundamentally settled in its current arrangements. Moves in, for example, Australia to abolish the role of the Queen in the country have met substantial opposition.

So, the Queen's place in the affections of her world seems assured. There is particularly widespread support for her grandsons, William and Harry.

These are young, media savvy princes, prepared to be seen in popular settings. Their links to injured war veterans has touched the hearts of the public.

Of course, the two are also the offspring of the much loved Princess Di. There have been times in recent years when the heir to the throne, the Prince of Wales, has appeared less well regarded.

However, his marriage to Camilla is now largely supported, perhaps a recognition that everybody deserves to find love.

The couple are particularly easy to work with, being approachable and flexible with many of the people whose role it is to support them.

Stories from Royal Residences

In addition to numerous properties on the Crown's estates, there are four main residences used by the Queen and Prince Philip. Two are owned directly by the Queen – Sandringham and Balmoral.

Buckingham Palace and Windsor Castle belong to the nation.

Buckingham Palace, her London address, was the scene of a famous security breach. In 1983 Michael Fagan entered the Palace after scaling the 14ft external wall.

He shinned up a drain pipe but was spotted by a maid, who alerted security. However by the time they arrived, Fagan was nowhere to be seen and the assumption was made that the maid was wrong.

In a catalogue of errors, the alarm sensors detected his movements once he entered the building, but another assumption was made – this time that the sensor was faulty.

Fagan, an out of work decorator, wandered around the home for 15 minutes, during which time he managed to break an ash tray and cut his hand.

At around 7.15am, he entered the Queen's bedroom and disturbed her when he brushed against a curtain.

Fagan claimed to sit on the Queen's bed, and she phoned twice for security, but with none arriving left the room.

A maid gave the intruder cigarettes before a duty footman, Paul Whybrew, arrived accompanied by police who removed Fagan.

It was a very British break in.

Fagan, whose wife had just left him, spent six months in a psychiatric hospital, before gaining further notoriety by recording a punk version of 'God Save the Queen'.

His mother later claimed that he had just broken in for a chat.

The intruder was ab;e to reach the Queen directly because a duty change to the armed security outside her bedroom was taking place, and no officer was present.

The Palace is no stranger to security breaches. It was the scene of a series of break ins during the 1800s. Edward Jones, known as 'the boy Jones' carried out the burglaries whilst still a teenager.

His story was the subject of a 1950 film, The Mudlark, which featured Sir Alec Guiness as the then Prime Minister Benjamin Disraeli.

Windsor Castle is a fine building, loved by many. Although close to London, and on the flightpath to nearby Heathrow, it's Great Park is a well-loved haunt of the Queen and other members of the Royal Family.

The Castle is often said to be her favourite home.

It also had personal appeal for Adolf Hitler who apparently earmarked it as his own residence should Britain be conquered during World War II.

Perhaps that is why the bombs avoided it.

The Queen's private Scottish home is Balmoral. Located in Royal Deeside, Aberdeenshire, the Castle has long been a favourite of royalty with its wonderful countryside.

It was first purchased by Prince Albert but his wife Victoria found it too cramped, and it was rebuilt, completion coming in 1856.

Tales of the Castle's haunted history are popular, with the story of John Brown one of the most popular.

Even the current Queen is reported as to having seen the alleged lover of her Great Grandmother.

The alleged relationship between Victoria and the kilt wearing servant was sufficiently notorious to make the big screen.

Brown was portrayed by Scottish comedian Billy Connolly, playing opposite Judi Dench's Victoria in the film, Mrs Brown.

There is also an official Scottish residence at the Palace of Holyroodhouse.

The last of the Queen's main residences is the Norfolk estate of Sandringham. This is the home to which the family retreat at Christmas.

Despite their love of a family get together, the number of royals has grown so much in recent years that the Queen cannot put them all up any longer.

In the same way as Joe Public has the stressful task of deciding who to invite and who to omit on the big day, so the Queen must make increasingly tricky decisions.

However, lunches during her stay can still be for up to 50, causing security to need crib sheets to check the identity of some of the lesser known family members.

Meals of this size, in what is – despite its outward appearance – an old fashioned house with many tiny rooms – at least mean that Christmas Dinner can be reserved for the immediate family.

However, just as we need to share out the Christmases by visiting different in-laws, so do Prince William and his wife, sometimes spending Christmas at the Middleton household in Buckinghamshire.

Finding appropriate gifts for people who have everything (except much time for relaxation) is tricky. Apparently, royals compete to find the funniest, tackiest gifts.

Perhaps visits to some of Norfolk's coastal attractions might provide inspiration?

What Next?

Now in their nineties, the Queen and, more so, Prince Philip are slowing down in their public lives.

Younger members of the Household are increasingly taking on responsibilities, for example, Prince Charles performs the majority of overseas commitments on behalf of his mother.

Princess Anne is another of the Queen's offspring renowned for her hard work in performing public duties.

We can only surmise at what the future might hold. The Queen Mother, Elizabeth Bowes-Lyon lived to 101, and remained very much a public figure well into her later years.

By contrast, her sister Margaret died at 71 and her father lived to just 56.

The public seem to have a growing fascination for younger members of the family, with enormous public and media attention given to the births of Prince George and Princess Charlotte.

Charles' sons are well regarded, with the younger, Harry, sometimes described as the public's favourite royal.

And although his father has caused controversy in the past, and has appeared to fall out of the population's favour, he is on a high at the moment.

We can only speculate. But whatever the future holds, we can count with great assurance that one person will remain in the hearts of the public.

Elizabeth Alexandra Mary Windsor, wife of Prince Philip, longest serving monarch in British history. Upholder of the faith, figure of unity, bringer of joy to so many.

Star of James Bond, mother, grandmother, great grandmother and, who knows, maybe one day great, great Grandmother is that person.

Made in the USA
Columbia, SC
02 December 2017